Biographies for Young Children

JULIETTE GORDON LOW

Founder of the Girl Scouts

Written by Shari Steelsmith
Illustrated by Connie J. Pope

Special thanks to the following children for their
help with the manuscript and illustrations:
Shannon Arneson, Peter Steelsmith, Stacy
Steelsmith, Brandy Fairchild, and the Girl Scout
Troop 1163, Totem Council, in Seattle, WA.

The author, illustrator, and publisher also thank
the Juliette Gordon Low Birthplace, Savannah,
GA, and the Girl Scouts of America, New York,
NY.

Published by:
Parenting Press, Inc.
P.O. Box 15163
Seattle, WA 98115

Dedicated to Brett Steelsmith and Christi Steelsmith Hartman

Most people now know me as Juliette, but everyone *I* knew called me
Daisy. I was born on Halloween 1860, and I arrived just in time for the Civil
War. Of course, we called it "The War between the States" back then. If
you lived in the North, you were called a Yankee. If you lived in the South,
you were called a Rebel.

I was a Rebel and so was my papa. Mama said he was the bravest
officer they'd ever had.

My mama was a Rebel too, even though most of her family were Yankees. When I was very small, the Yankee Army marched through Savannah, where we lived.

One Yankee general came to visit. I went right up to the soldier with him and asked, "What happened to your arm?"

"Got it shot off by a Rebel," he answered.

"My papa prob'ly did it," I told him. "He's shot lots of Yankees."

The soldier just laughed.

Things were dangerous in Savannah with the Yankees there. One of my uncles came to take us to Chicago, to wait for the end of the war. Mama didn't want to go. But she knew we'd be safer in the North.

I don't remember much about Chicago, except for the stories my grandmother told me. My favorite was about my great-grandmother, Eleanor Lytle Kinzie. She was captured by Seneca Indians when she was only a young girl. The Indians grew to love her and adopted her into their family. They called her "*Little-Ship-Under-Full-Sail.*"

"Why did they call her that?" I asked.

"Because she was so determined," said Grandmother Juliette. "When she wanted to do something, no matter how hard it was, she got the job done. Your mother is like her, and so are you, Daisy. After a few years, Eleanor was able to return to her own family. She never forgot her friends among the Indians."

I always remembered the story of *Little-Ship-Under-Full-Sail.* Imagine being so determined that you could make friends with people who spoke another language!

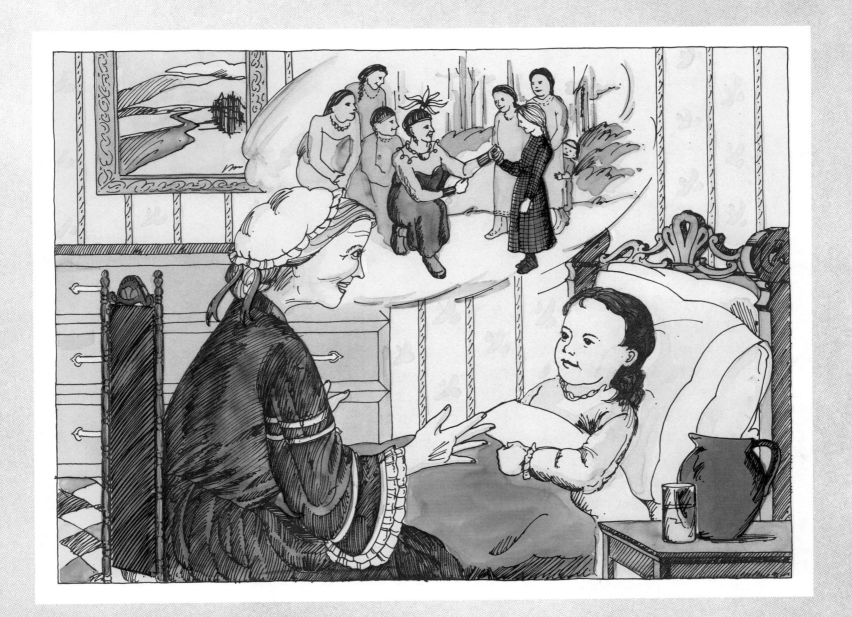

While we were in Chicago, we heard the bad news. We had lost the war! We had to wait a while before we could go home to Savannah. My sisters and I were happy to see that our house was all right, and so was the house next door where our cousins lived! There were three of us Gordons, and then all the Anderson cousins besides.

One time we had a taffy pull. Cousin Randolph helped me pull the candy. It was a warm, honey-brown color. He looked at it and then at me. "Look Daisy," he said. "It's the *exact* same color as your hair!"

I held some taffy up against my braid. "I'll bet no one would notice if we braided some taffy into it," I said. Mama saw it right away, but the candy had already hardened. She scolded me something dreadful as she cut it out of my hair.

Oh well, I thought, sometimes it seems like my ideas get ahead of my common sense. Then I smiled. Trying new things was risky, but it was too exciting to give up.

During the summers, my brothers and sisters and cousins and I went to my aunt's plantation, Etowah Cliffs.

I had a lot of good ideas at Etowah Cliffs. One time, my sister Nellie and I made up a secret recipe for a drink called "Peach Gobble." We sold it to the other cousins for paper money. My little sister Alice loved Etowah Cliffs too.

Summer didn't last forever. I did have to go to school. When I was fourteen, I went away to a boarding school in Virginia called Stuart Hall.

Then I went to another boarding school in New York City. We could only speak French there. Can you imagine? It was hard at first, but I remembered my great-grandmother *Little-Ship-Under-Full-Sail.* If she could learn to speak an Indian language, I could certainly learn French!

Before I graduated, my sister Alice caught scarlet fever and died. No one I really loved had died before this. I didn't know I would miss her so much.

When I was 22, I decided it was time to see the world! I went to England first. I stayed with some family friends, the Lows. I liked the daughters Katy, Hattie, and Amy. I liked their brother Willy so much that, in a few years, we became engaged.

I loved going to see people and making new friends. I felt like the world was an exciting place to be. Until that is, I had a bad ear infection. I went to see a doctor in Savannah. I had read about a new silver nitrate treatment in the newspaper, and I suggested he try it.

"Are you sure you want to try this, Miss Gordon?" he asked.

"Of course, I do," I insisted, "I'm sure it will work."

It did *not* work. The treatment made it worse. Blood came out of my ear. I couldn't even stand up. When I finally got better, most of my hearing in that ear was gone. Like I said, sometimes my good ideas didn't work out so well.

Things got even worse. After our wedding, when Willy and I were leaving, people threw "good luck rice" at us. One grain of rice lodged in my good ear. It started an infection and I was sick in bed *again*. After I got better, almost all of my hearing was gone.

I felt bad about it, of course. But I also felt that problems should be faced. I carried on, just like my great-grandmother *Little-Ship-Under-Full-Sail.*

A hearing aid helped some. Then Willy and I moved to his house in England. I loved giving parties, and most of our guests went hunting with us. Willy and I even visited Buckingham Palace to see Queen Victoria.

I kept travelling and making friends. France, India, and Egypt were all fun, but Savannah was my favorite place to visit. Wherever I went, I always took my dogs and my parrot, Polly Poons.

In 1898 the Spanish-American War broke out. I heard my papa was a brigadier general. Mama followed Papa to Miami to organize a hospital for sick soldiers. I caught the next ship to America. I wanted to help with the hospital.

Many soldiers were sick with typhoid fever. My job in the hospital was to work in the kitchen. The cooking was hot, sticky work.

We never had enough food, especially milk. I made it my job to go out looking for more. I would talk to farmers and tell them about the sick soldiers. Sometimes I'd find myself in a pasture, milking a friendly cow. I put the milk in buckets. I never came back empty-handed. I found that a person with a lot of ideas can be helpful just about anywhere.

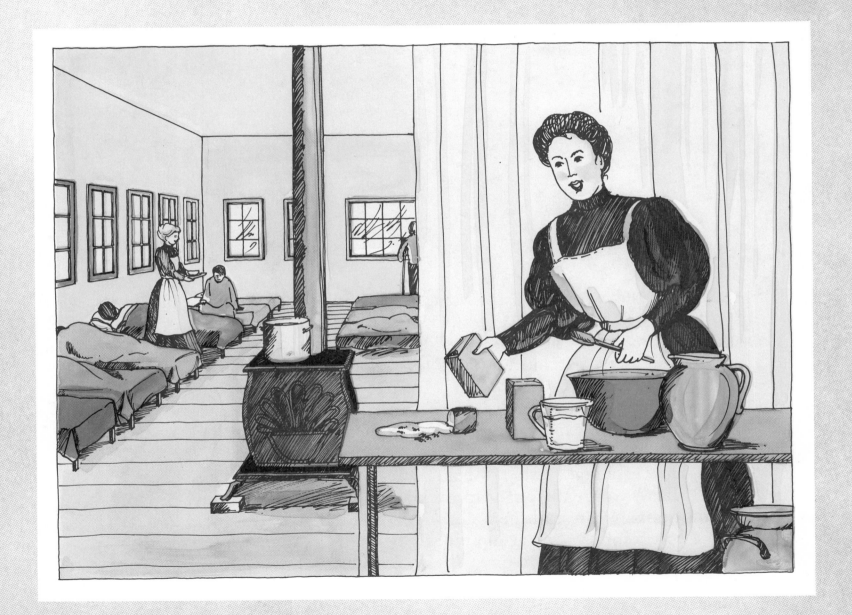

After the war was over, I went back to England. My husband Willy was sick, and in 1905 he died. I felt very sad and lonely. For the first time in my 45 years I couldn't think of any good ideas.

After some searching, I found my new project. I met a man named Sir Robert Baden-Powell. He had recently founded a new group called the Boy Scouts. They learned outdoor and survival skills like tracking and exploring. He was full of energy, and I caught some of it.

"How exciting!" I said. "I would love to teach girls scouting!"

"Daisy, you really ought to round up some girls and start a group," he suggested. "We call them Girl Guides here."

I was inspired. My group quickly learned first aid, map reading, signalling, knots, and cooking. I just knew girls all over the world would love scouting. I began to plan. Then I caught a ship for America.

As soon as I reached Savannah, I phoned my old and dear friend, Nina Pape.

"Come right over," I said. "I've got something for the girls of Savannah, and all America, and all the world. And we're going to start it tonight."

I explained to Nina about scouting and guiding. It could help girls learn how to take care of themselves in the woods, explore new things, and above all, help others in need.

"This is exactly what I've tried to do with my life," I said. "I know I can help young girls do these things."

Now all the friends I had made over the years in my travelling came in handy. I went from city to city and talked to everyone I could think of. Girls signed up right and left. I set up troops and found leaders. This was my best idea yet.

When World War I began, my Girl Scouts had a chance to help with the war effort. Even though I was starting to be tired and sick a lot, I went with my Girl Scouts to help in hospitals and canteens. I was so proud of those girls.

After the war ended, we all thought more about peace. My own ancestors had worked hard to bring peace to the American frontier. *Little-Ship-Under-Full-Sail* had done her best to understand her Seneca Indian friends. Why couldn't my Girl Scouts meet and understand girls from other countries? I helped set up "World Camps" where Girl Scouts and Girl Guides from all over the world could meet to promote peace and goodwill.

The American Girl Scouts' first camp was named after me--Camp Juliette Low on Lookout Mountain in Georgia. The first campout was exciting. If you have a campfire, you have to tell stories. And I was one of the best storytellers around. The girls' favorite story was my favorite too--*Little-Ship-Under-Full-Sail.*

My favorite memory of camps with the Girl Scouts was in 1926. That's when we had a World Camp. Girls from countries everywhere came to our camp in New York. Although I was sick with cancer at the time, I enjoyed every minute.

The girls from Holland gave me a doll that I carried around with me. We told stories from our own countries around the fire at night. I was glad to see the girls making friends. "It's a step toward peace," I thought.

I once wrote a letter to all the Girl Scouts on my birthday. I said:

As you gather to celebrate our Girl Scout week in November, think of the girls around the world who are your sister Girl Scouts and Girl Guides. We can make scouting so much a part of our everyday life that people will recognize the Girl Scout spirit and say, "Why, of course. She is a Girl Scout."

And that is how I hope people will remember me.

INTRODUCING THE DECISION IS YOURS SERIES

These are fun books that help children age 7-11 think about social problems. Written in the "choose your own ending" format, the reader gets to decide what action the character will take and then gets to see the consequences of that decision.

These books:

- Address social issues, like stealing, jealousy, and lying, that affect 7-11 year olds.
- Encourage children to think about consequences.
- Help children develop and practice problem solving skills.
- Offer children a chance to see why some things work and some things don't.

FINDERS KEEPERS
by Elizabeth Crary

You and your friend Jerry are walking home from the pool on a hot summer day. You find a wallet lying under a tree — it belongs to your neighbor, Mr. French. Jerry wants to take a little money and buy ice cream. You're not sure what to do. Will you keep it? Will you turn it in? Will you go with Jerry to buy ice cream?

$3.95 paper,   64 pages, illustrated
ISBN 0-943990-38-6

BULLY ON THE BUS
by Carl W. Bosch

You had an argument with a big kid named Nick on the bus. Now Nick wants to beat you up. You don't want to fight, but you are tired of being hassled all the time. Your mom thinks you should ignore him and your best friend thinks you should move to Texas. You're not so sure either will work. What *will* you do?

$3.95 paper,   64 pages, illustrated
ISBN 0-943990-42-4

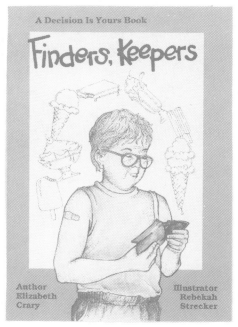

A Decision Is Yours Book

Finders, Keepers

Author
Elizabeth
Crary

Illustrator
Rebekah
Strecker

A DECISION IS YOURS BOOK

BULLY on the bus

Written by Carl W. Bosch
Illustrated by Rebekah J. Strecker

6

You ask Jerry to give you the wallet so you can 7 take it to the pool. He says, "No!" You grab for the wallet and knock it from his hand.

Before you can pick up the wallet, Jerry is standing with one foot on it. He flaps his arms like a bird and chants, "Chicken, chicken! You are a chicken! You are a chicken!"

You are not sure what to do. Jerry says, "Come on, it won't hurt you to look. I'm not going to take anything."

If you decide to give it to the Lost and Found, turn to page 5.

If you are curious to see if there is any money, turn to page 9.

THE BIOGRAPHIES FOR YOUNG CHILDREN SERIES

Children make their decisions about male/female roles between the ages of 3-6. Because these ideas are formed so early, it is important for children to have examples of strong people who chose non-traditional roles and changed society. These picture-story books are fun and riveting for preschoolers and are simple enough for an eight year old to read alone.

HARRIET TUBMAN: They Called Me Moses
by Linda Meyer
illustrated by J. Kerstetter

Harriet Tubman is probably the best remembered ''conductor'' on the Underground Railroad during the Civil War. The drama and adventure in her story will fascinate young children. Narrated by Harriet herself as a child.

$5.95 paper   32 pages, illustrated
ISBN 0-943990-32-7

COMING SOON:
KATHARINE LEE BATES: Author of ''America the Beautiful''

ELIZABETH BLACKWELL: The Story of the First Woman Doctor
by Shari Steelsmith
illustrated by J. Kerstetter

Children will be interested to read about Elizabeth Blackwell's unusual childhood, fierce determination to become a doctor, hard work, various setbacks, and eventual success. Told from Elizabeth's viewpoint as a child.

$5.95, paper   32 pages, illustrated
ISBN 0-943990-30-0

Order Form

Bully on the Bus	$3.95	_____
Finders, Keepers	$3.95	_____
Elizabeth Blackwell	$5.95	_____
Harriet Tubman	$5.95	_____

Shipping

Order Subtotal	Shipping		
$ 0-$10	add $2.00	Subtotal	_____
$10-$25	add $3.00	Shipping	_____
$25-$50	add $4.00	*Sales Tax	_____
		Total	_____